NOW YOU SEE IT, NOW YOU DON'T

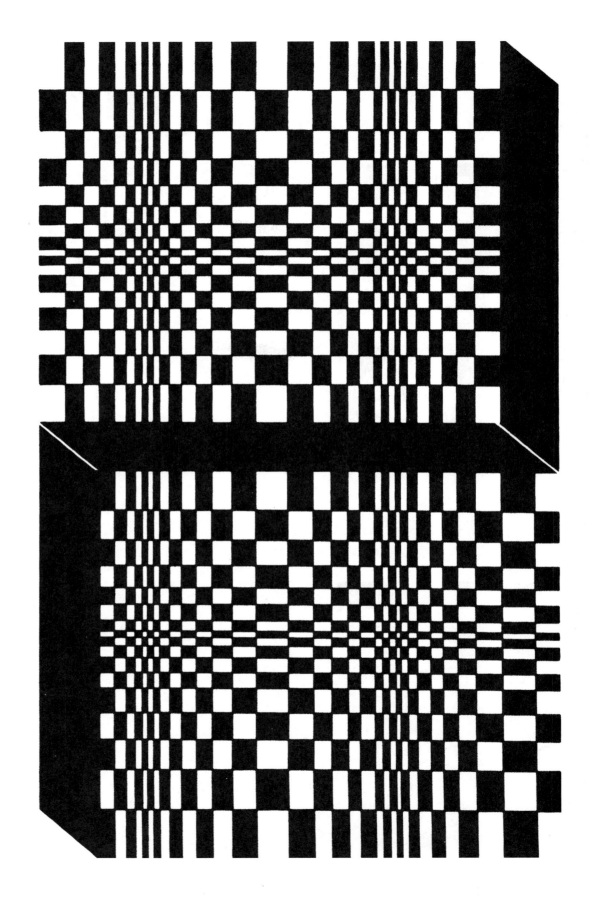

NOW YOU SEE IT, NOW YOU DON'T

The Amazing World of Optical Illusions

SEYMOUR SIMON

DRAWINGS BY CONSTANCE FTERA

REVISED EDITION

Morrow Junior Books
New York

Previous edition published as *The Optical Illusion Book*

For Joyce with love

Photo Credits: Wide World Photos, page 36. Color insert art, in order of appearance: © 1998 IllusionWorks, L.L.C. All Rights Reserved; Reutersvärd © 1998; Photo Researchers, Inc. © Porterfield/Chickering; © 1998 IllusionWorks, L.L.C. All Rights Reserved; © 1998 IllusionWorks, L.L.C. All Rights Reserved; © 1998 IllusionWorks, L.L.C. All Rights Reserved; © 1998 IllusionWorks, L.L.C. All Rights Reserved; Photograph by Susan Schwartzenberg, © 1984, The Exploratorium.

Published by Morrow Junior Books
a division of William Morrow and Company, Inc.
1350 Avenue of the Americas, New York, NY 10019
www.williammorrow.com

Printed in the United States of America.

1   2   3   4   5   6   7   8   9   10

Library of Congress Cataloging-in-Publication Data
Simon, Seymour.
Now you see it, now you don't: the amazing world of optical illusions / by Seymour Simon.
p.   cm.
Previously published in 1976.
Includes index.
ISBN 0-688-16152-9
1. Optical illusions—Juvenile literature.   I. Title.
QP495.S57 1998   152.14'8—DC21   97-49855   CIP

CONTENTS

o you believe everything you see? Are you sure? Look at the two straight lines in the figure at the left. Which is longer, line AB or line CD?

It may look as if line CD is longer. But is it really? You'll need a ruler to tell for sure. Measure each line. Both lines are the same length, even though one *looks* longer.

Now look at the figure below. Which line is longer, AB or BC? Measure each line with your ruler. Surprised? Both lines are exactly the same length.

You have been looking at two optical, or visual, illusions. An optical illusion is something you see that is not exactly what is really there. One line seems to be longer than another even though both are actually the same length.

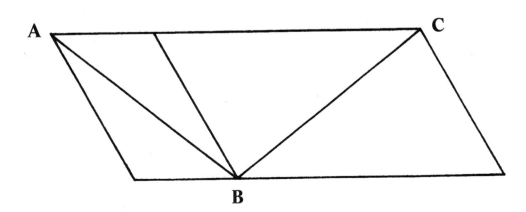

There are many different kinds of optical illusions. Some you see each day in nature, such as the way the sun or moon appears to move when clouds float by. Other illusions are done purposefully to fool you, such as the way artists make you see distance in a flat drawing.

Look at the three telegraph poles. When you see them without any background, they are the same size. But look what happens when you place a few simple lines in the background. Now which telegraph pole looks biggest?

To make them appear to be the same size, the artist has to draw each pole a different size. By doing this, the artist produces an illusion of distance in a picture that is really flat, like in the illustration to the right.

You will see many optical illusions in this book. You'll also discover why you see them the way you do. Show them to your friends. It's fun to share in the illusion of seeing and not believing.

Just to show you that everything may not be so simple to figure out, look at the drawing below. Can you see where the three prongs come from? Try drawing the figure on another sheet of paper. Even if you can draw it, you may not believe it!

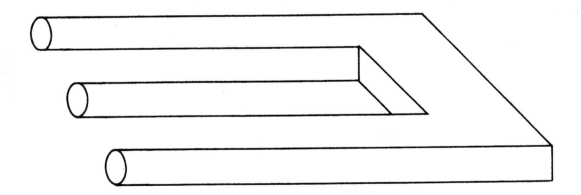

It is not just your eyes that let you see. You see because of the cooperation of nerve cells in your eyes with nerve cells in your brain, and the connection between them called the *optic nerve.*

Your eye is shaped like a small ball about one inch across. It sits in a cuplike socket in the front of your head. Your eyelids hide part of your eye and make it appear oval-shaped. Four sets of small muscles hold your eyeball in its socket. The muscles make your eye move side to side and up and down.

A cross section of your eye looks something like the illustration on page 10. The *cornea* is a clear, protective covering. It lets in light, but keeps out dust and other harmful things. Just behind the cornea is the *lens.* The lens focuses the light coming into your eye. The light forms an image that falls on the *retina.*

The amount of light coming into your eye is regulated by the *iris*, which is the colored part of your eye. The iris opens and closes, depending on the brightness of the light. The black dot in the center of the iris is where the light enters. It is called the *pupil.*

Here is what happens when you look at something, say a pencil in your hand. Light reflected from the pencil and your hand enters your eye through your pupil. The lens forms the light into an image that is a small picture of the pencil in your hand. The image falls upside down on the retina.

The retina contains more than one hundred million sensitive nerve cells. When light strikes the retina, the nerve cells respond. They send out tiny electric currents called *nerve impulses.*

The impulses travel along the cells to the optic nerve. The nerve cells that make up the optic nerve carry the impulses to the cells in the brain.

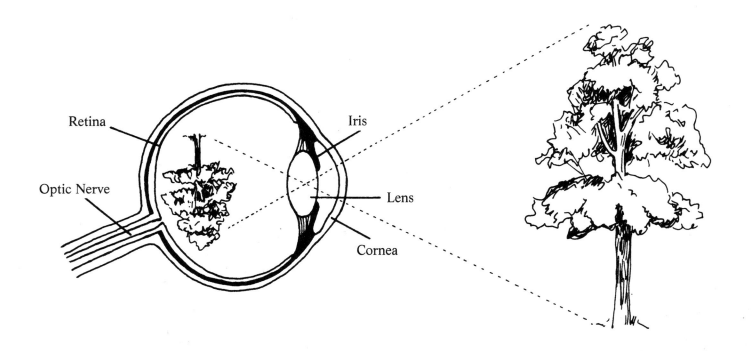

It is in your mind that the act of seeing finally takes place. Your brain puts together the nerve impulses from your eyes along with impulses from other cells in your brain. All these interacting impulses become the picture that you see.

We still don't know exactly how the brain works. We are not sure how patterns of nerve impulses are created and why they remain or change. We don't know where the brain stores its previous information. But scientists are now working on many of these questions. Perhaps we will soon begin to learn some of these answers. And no doubt, the answers will, in turn, lead to new questions.

Some interesting experiments already have been done on the nature of seeing. For example, we know that an electric shock or a blow to certain parts of your head can cause you to see lights. *(Do not try it. It can cause severe injury.)* This goes along with the expression that a person "sees stars" when hit on the head. The cells on the retina will release nerve impulses just as if they had been stimulated by light rays.

By the way, there is one spot on the retina that is not sensitive to light. It is called the *blind spot.* It is located at the point where the optic nerve enters the retina. Each of your eyes has a blind spot.

Normally, you are not aware of the blind spots. Your eyes are constantly shifting around. They will provide you with enough information about the scene you are looking at so that you will not notice the blind spot.

But there is an easy way to become aware of the blind spot in your eye. Look at the X below. Close your left eye. Hold this book at arm's length and look straight at the X with your right eye. Keep staring straight at the X while you slowly bring the book closer to your eye. At some point, about six to ten inches from your eye, you will no longer see the dot to the side of the X. If you bring the book closer, the dot will appear again. At the point that you can't see the dot, the light from it falls just on the blind spot.

If you want to check the blind spot in your left eye, turn the book over. Now close your right eye. Stare directly at the X with your left eye and follow the same directions.

In the next chapter, you will look at several ways that your eyes and your brain can come to a mistaken conclusion about what you are seeing.

X   •

inding out why you see an optical illusion may not be very easy. For example, the figure at the top right is the first optical illusion you saw in this book.

You already know that both lines are the same length, even though line CD looks longer. Try showing this illusion to your friends and classmates. Almost all of them will see line CD as the longer one.

At one time, people explained the illusion with a theory that it was more difficult to raise your eyes upward a certain distance than to move them sideward the same distance. But this explanation doesn't hold up when it is investigated more carefully. For one thing, it hasn't been proven that it's more difficult to move your eyes upward. Furthermore, no one has shown that the difficulty would make the line seem longer.

Would you like to disprove the theory yourself? Draw the figure sideways, like the figure below right.

Which line looks longer now? Ask your friends. Most of them will think that CD still looks longer. But line CD is now sideways. So the explanation about the difficulty in moving your eyes upward as opposed to sideward doesn't seem to work.

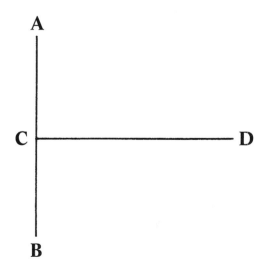

Another explanation for this illusion seems to hold up better. The reason line AB seems shorter is because line CD interrupts it. For example, most people see no illusion if the lines interrupt each other equally, as in the two figures to the left.

But if the lines interrupt each other at different points, as they do in the two figures below, the illusion comes back.

So perhaps this newer theory is the correct one. But we can't be sure. In science, we believe a theory only if it helps explain the evidence. When new evidence comes up that the theory cannot explain, we must develop a new theory.

The figures to the right are two more illusions. The two horizontal lines are equal in length in both drawings, even though the top ones look longer.

The theory about what makes this illusion work goes by the name of *perspective*. In real life, you can see this illusion if you look down a highway or a railway track. The sides of the road or the track seem to come together in the distance. An artist uses this idea when he or she wants you to see depth in a scene that's been drawn on a flat surface.

Try these illusions on your friends. Most of us have seen lines like this so often in drawings and photographs that we accept the narrowing part as being farther away. Even though your eye sees the two horizontal lines as equal in length, your brain uses other information to interpret what you see. Using previous experience with perspective, it decides that the top line is farther away than the bottom line. It then concludes that a farther object that appears to be the same size as a closer object must actually be larger. Of course, you are not conscious of this process in your brain. You are only aware of the result. To you, the top line just looks longer.

Even if all your friends see the same illusion, not everybody in the world is fooled. As you might guess, people who have no experience with perspective in drawings or photographs would not see this illusion.

Scientists tried out these illusions on some people in the African country Uganda. The Ugandans who lived in

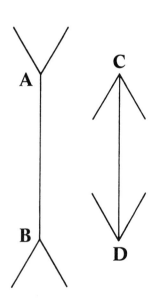

cities and had experience with drawings and photographs were fooled by the illusion. The Ugandans who lived in the back country and had never seen perspective drawings or photographs were not fooled. They saw the two lines as equal in length.

You can understand that it is not only your eyes that see an optical illusion. The way you see things has a lot to do with your previous experience. That helps explain why not everyone sees the same optical illusions.

This theory about the importance of previous experience can be supported by still another illusion. It is called the Muller-Lyer illusion, after the scientist who discovered it, and is shown in the two sets of figures on this page.

Which lines look longer to you, AB or CD? Use a ruler to prove that both lines are really the same length. Ask your friends to look at these drawings. Most likely, all of them will agree with you that line AB seems longer than CD.

Does everyone around the world see this illusion? Again, scientists found that some people do not. Certain African tribespeople who had little contact with modern technology saw the illusion while other tribes did not. What could be the reason?

Here is the theory that seems to help explain why some peoples see the illusion and others don't. The Muller-Lyer drawings look to you something like the edges of buildings or boxes or other square objects. Look at the drawings to the right, for example.

You are used to seeing drawings of things in perspective. So you *think* that line AB, which appears to be farther away and yet the same length as the closer line CD, must actually be longer. That's why the Muller-Lyer illusion works for you.

Some African tribes have round houses and doors with curved edges. They have no boxes and rarely see anything that has a right-angle edge. They also do not use perspective in their art and are not familiar with photographs. According to the theory, these facts help explain why these tribes are not fooled by the Muller-Lyer illusion.

It seems more and more certain that this theory is correct. You see many illusions not because your eyes see them but because your brain uses previous experiences to interpret what your eyes see.

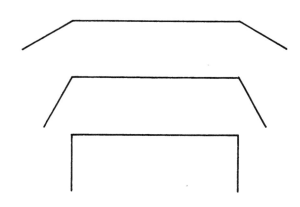

One of the most interesting things about this optical illusion is that you can draw equal lines yet still see them as unequal. Start by drawing three horizontal lines, all the same length, as in the figure at the top. They look equal in length at this point.

Now add vertical or slanting lines to the ends of each line just as in the figure at the bottom. The added lines change the way we see the three horizontal lines. The top line seems longer than the middle line, and the middle line seems longer than the bottom line. This is so even though you know you drew the lines equal in length.

The reason for this illusion again seems to deal with perspective. That is, the more the end lines slant, the farther away the horizontal lines seem to be. Because of this, the top line seems farthest away. But the top horizontal line is the same length as the middle and bottom lines. So your brain concludes that a line farther away that appears to be the same length as a closer one must really be longer.

You can destroy this illusion just by rearranging the order of the lines, as in the lower figure on page 19.

Now you no longer have any perspective in the drawing. One line doesn't seem any farther away than another line. So all the lines that are equal will seem equal.

Sometimes you can consciously change the way an illusion appears to you. Look back at the bottom figure on this page. Try to pay no attention to the top line. Look at the middle and the bottom horizontal lines. Soon you should be able to make them look equal.

The figure to the right is another drawing that you can change if you study it for a while. Is line B or C a continuation of line A? At first line C looks like the continuation. But place a ruler or other straightedge on the figure. You can see that line B is really the continuation of line A. Remove the ruler and you can probably force yourself to see the lines correctly. Still another way to see the figure correctly is to turn the book until lines A, B, and C are horizontal. That destroys the illusion.

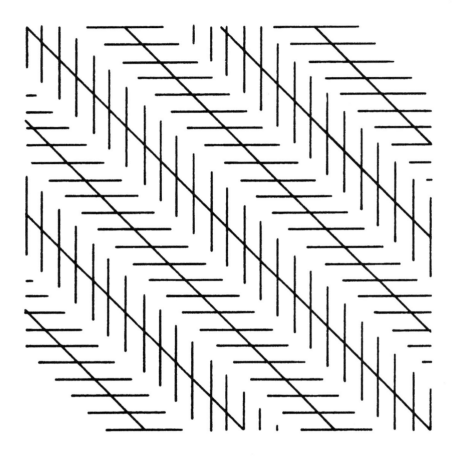

Another illusion that you can change by shifting your point of view is the figure above. The long lines look as if they slant toward each other. But hold the book up to your eye. Turn the book sideways and sight along the long lines. The short crossing lines are no longer easy to see. The long lines now look parallel to each other. Again perspective seems to play a part in this optical illusion.

Here are some drawings that may not be so easy for you to see correctly no matter how you hold them. In the two figures below, both circles are the same size.

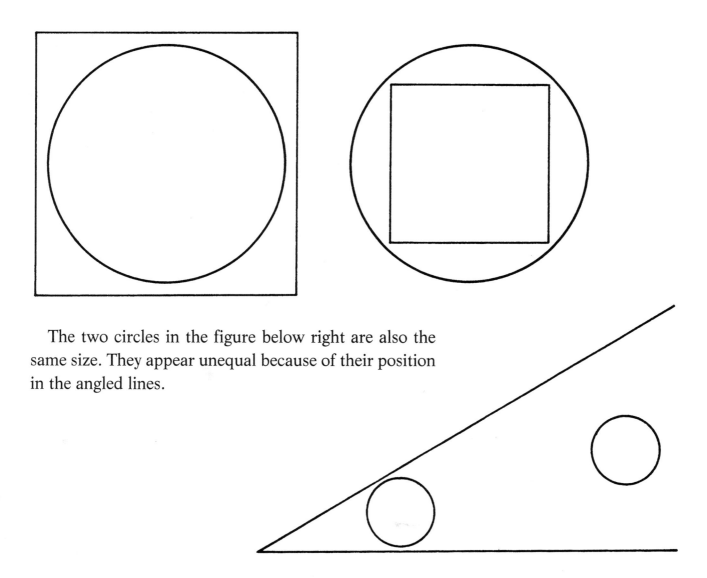

The two circles in the figure below right are also the same size. They appear unequal because of their position in the angled lines.

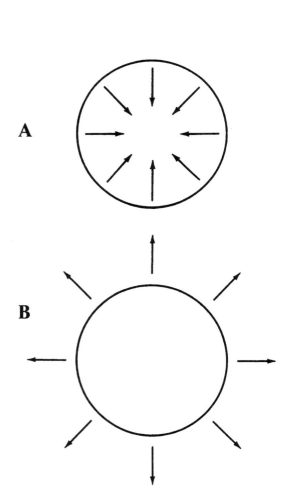

The figure above has equal-sized circles that appear unequal because of the surrounding circles. The center circles are both the same size. The one on the right seems larger because you compare it to the surrounding smaller circles. The one on the left seems smaller because you compare it to the surrounding larger circles.

The two circles in the figure to the left are also equal in size. The arrows within circle A seem to pull it inward and make the circle appear smaller. The arrows outside circle B seem to pull it outward and make the circle appear larger.

Sometimes a circle doesn't even seem like a circle because of its surroundings. In the figure to the left, the circle appears to pull in at each point that it intersects the inside square.

In the figure to the right, the circles appear distorted. The background pattern of slanting lines causes this effect.

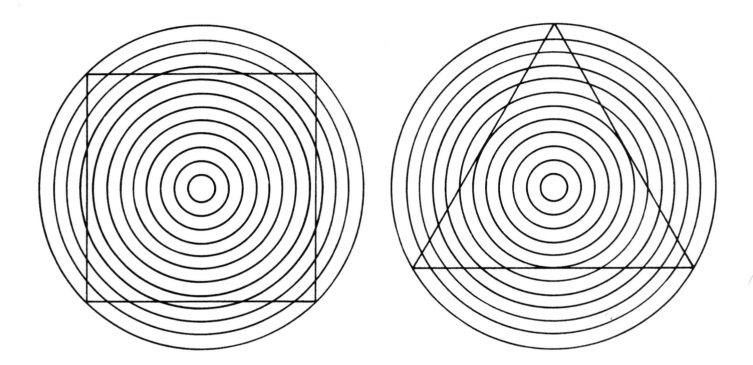

You can also use circles to make straight lines appear to bend. The figure to the left is really a square against a background of circles. The sides of the square appear to bend inward because of the pulling effect of the circles on your eyes.

The triangle in the figure to the right has straight-line sides. Again the circles make the lines appear to bend inward.

Even parts of a circle can make a straight line seem to bend. Look at the figure above.

Sometimes parts of the same circle don't seem to have the same curve. The figure to the right shows three arcs of the same circle. The differences in their lengths appear to make each arc curve differently. Place the edge of a cutout paper circle over each arc, and you will see that they are alike.

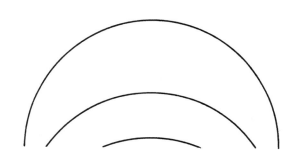

The figure below shows some circles that look like spirals. To prove that they are circles, trace one of them out with a compass.

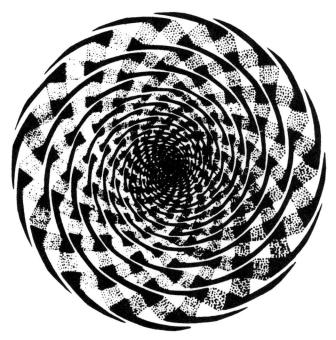

Even the direction in which you look at a drawing may make it appear different. These two squares are the same size. The one on the left looks larger because you view it as a diamond when it is tilted.

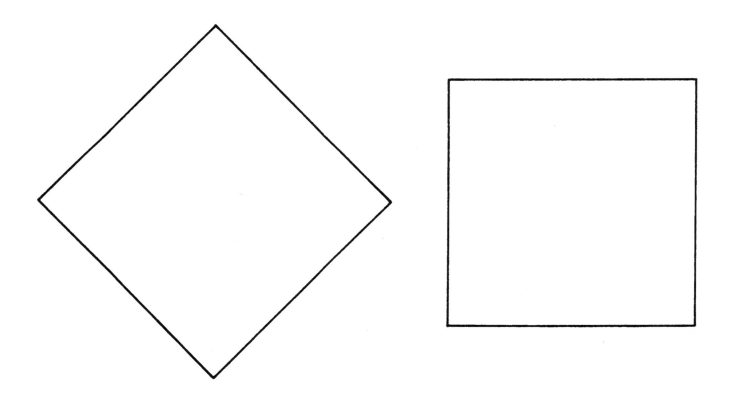

There are many different ways that lines and spaces can be arranged to make you see illusions. In the next chapter, you will see some illusions that continue to change as you look at them.

Here's an illusion that changes back and forth as you look at it. Is the bent card shown in the figure to the right facing toward you or away from you? You should be able to make it flip back and forth every few seconds.

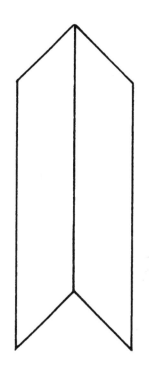

The card seems to change easily because there is no reason to see it one way rather than another. Either way you see it makes equally good sense to you. The figure below is another drawing that you can see equally well in two different positions. It's called a reversing cube. Do you see the area bounded by the darker lines as the outside surface of a transparent box? Keep looking, and the bounded area will become the inner surface of a box tilted in a different way. Now see if you can make it flip back and forth.

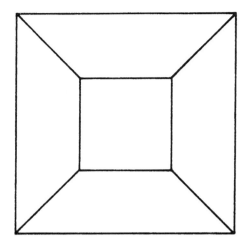

Does the center square of the figure to the left project toward you or away from you? Or does it do both?

Look at the figure in the middle. Which way does the staircase run? Keep looking, and it will reverse in front of your eyes. If you don't see the reversal, think of one edge of a step as first nearer and then farther away.

Do the rings in the figure at the bottom show a hollow tube running from left to right or from right to left? Keep looking at the figure. Rapidly close and open each eye one at a time. What happens every time you blink an eye?

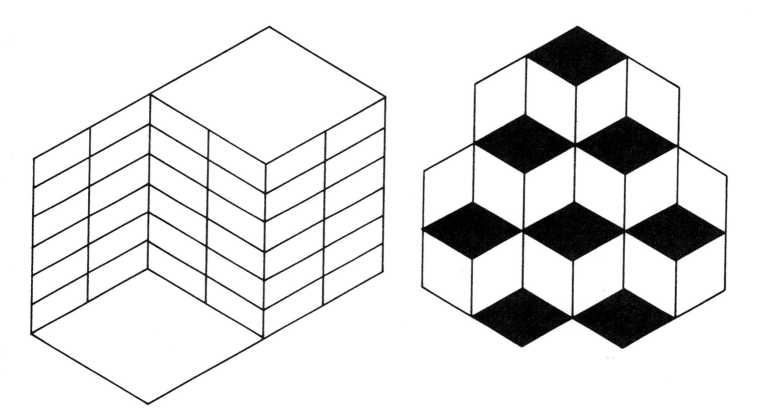

Do you see the figure to the left as a solid figure with one long edge, or do you see it as two solid figures leaning on each other? Keep looking to make it change from one to the other.

The drawing of boxes in the figure to the right may not seem to stay still long enough to be counted. Do you see six or seven stacked boxes? View the black diamonds as either the tops or the bottoms of the boxes.

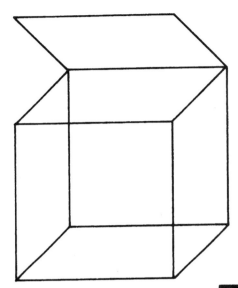

The figure to the left is a single box. The trouble with this box is that the lid is either open toward you or away from you. Which way do you see it? Keep looking to make it switch from one to the other.

Sometimes it's difficult to tell which is the object and which is the background. Look at the figure below. Do you see this as white lines on a black background or black lines on a white background?

Which is the figure and which is the background in the drawing above? Do you see two faces staring at each other or a lovely vase?

At times, your brain has to supply missing information in a drawing. The figure to the right is a bunch of oddly shaped black spots. Use your imagination to see a dog. (Would you call the dog "Spot"?)

Do you see anything in the black spots in the figure below left? (Would you believe a horse and rider?)

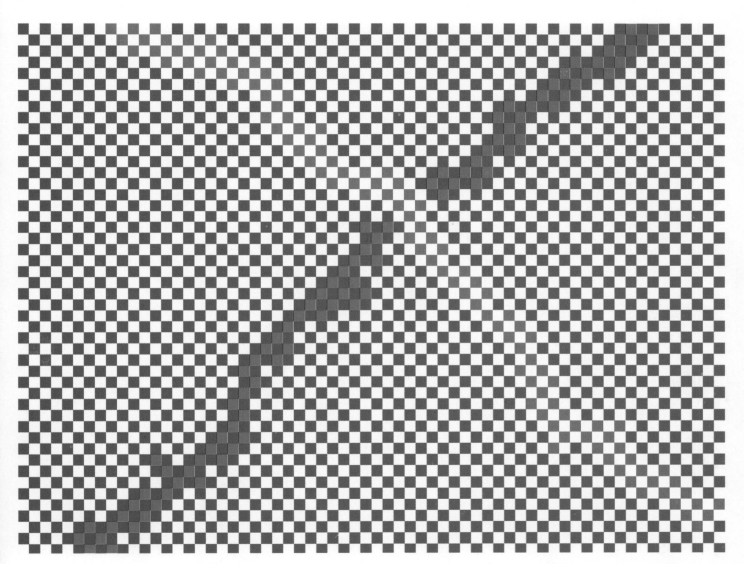

It looks as if the two crossing lines are different colors, but, in fact, both are the same. The difference is that one of the arms has pink squares against a background of white squares and the other arm has the same color pink squares against a background of green squares.

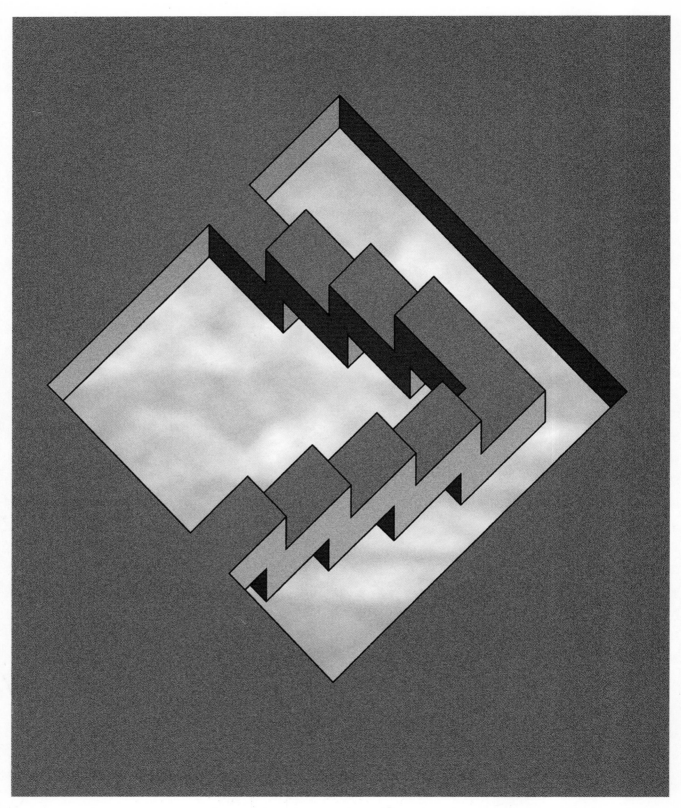

The stairs seem to go down and up, but somehow they end on the same level either way.

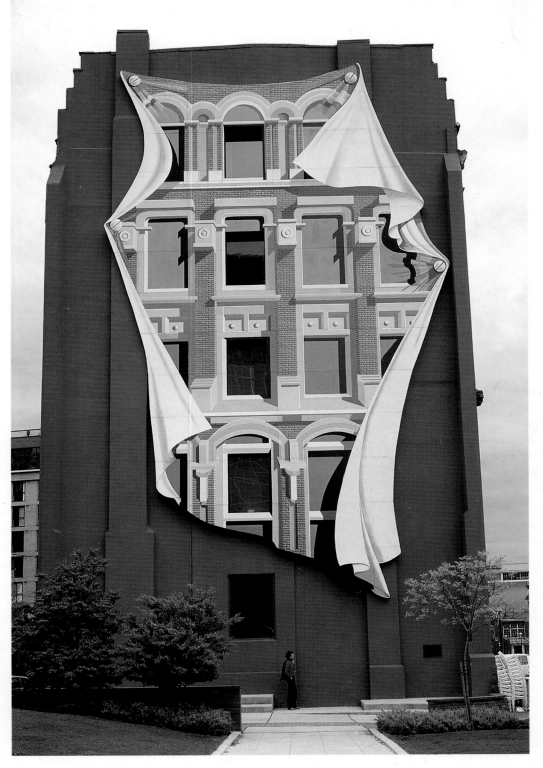

Here, a painting of a building seems to be tacked up on an actual building.
Which looks more real to you—the painting or the actual building?

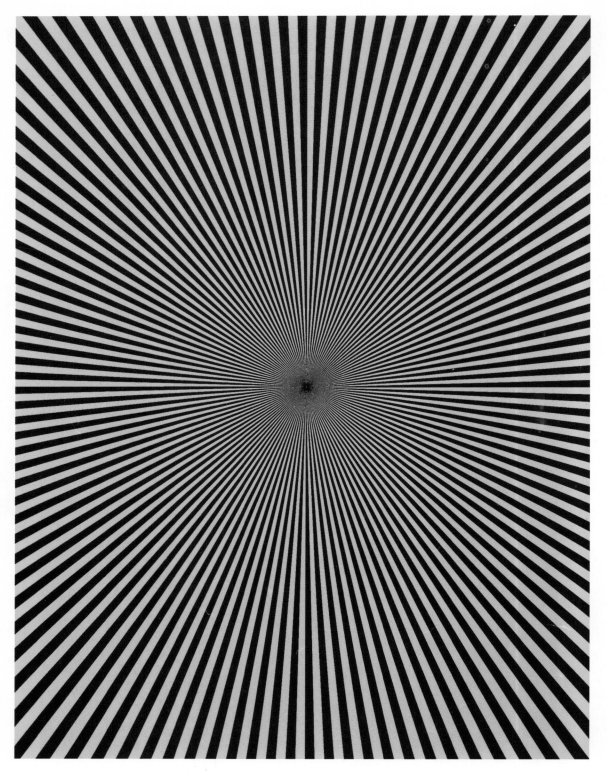

These lines look as if they are pulsating and rippling, but of course they are really standing still. The colors in the painting are yellow and black, but you may see other colors as well. The moving lines and the mysterious colors are all in your mind!

Stare at the red parrot for thirty seconds. Then look immediately at the empty bird cage. You may see a faint, ghostly image of a blue-green bird in the cage. Try the same with the green bird, and you may see a faint purplish bird in the cage.

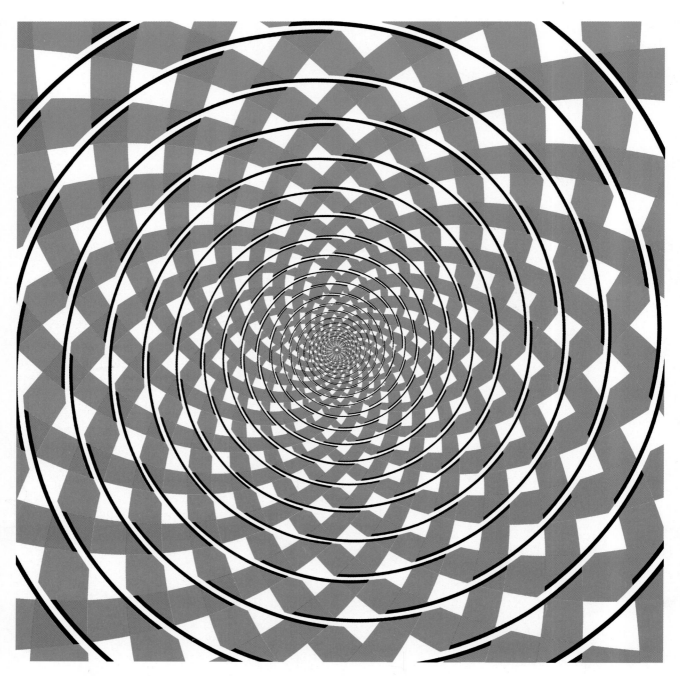

You may think you are looking at a spiral, but trace each of the spiral lines with your finger. The spiral lines are really circles.

Are the thick black lines and the open spaces between them exactly parallel to one another?
Look again.

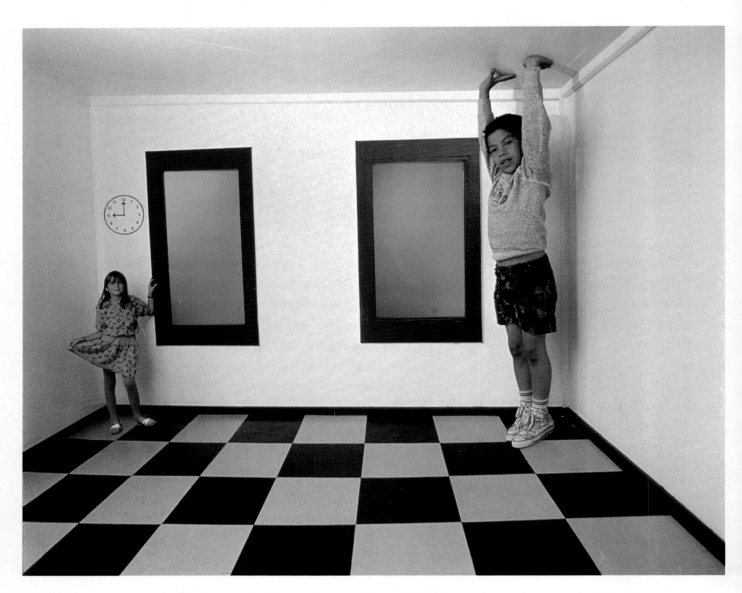

A giant person and a tiny person in the same room? Not at all. Both people are the same size. It's the room that has been constructed so that the ceiling on one side is much lower than the ceiling on the other side. The boy on the side of the room that has the lower ceiling seems to be huge. The girl on the side of the room that has the higher ceiling seems to be tiny by comparison.

When a drawing becomes more complicated, it can cause you to see images that are really quite different from each other. For example, do you see a duck or a rabbit in the drawing to the right?

Do you see a pretty young girl or an old witch in the lower drawing to the right? (The young girl's chin becomes the witch's nose.)

Sometimes extra information in a drawing makes us see it one way or another. The illustration below shows two sketches of a face. One seems to be looking straight at you, while the other seems to be looking over your shoulder. But cover the bottom halves of both faces. Keep looking at both pairs of eyes. If you try, you can make both pairs of eyes seem to look directly at you. When you uncover the bottom of the drawing, the eyes of the person on the left shift back.

In this figure do you see black arrows pointing left and right? Or do you see white arrows pointing up and down?

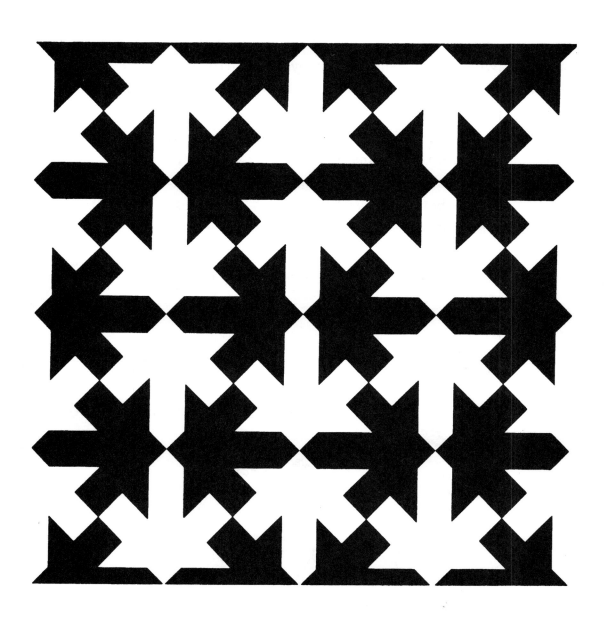

The figure below shows some groups of dots. In the first group, the dots seem to be arranged in columns. In the second group, the dots seem to be arranged in lines. In the third group, you can see the dots as either columns or lines. The third group is a changeable figure. Can you see the differences in the arrangements and number of dots in the three groups? Do you understand why a changeable figure can be viewed in different ways?

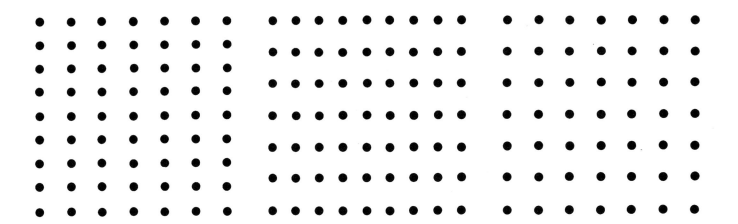

5 | Depth and Distance

ook at this photograph. Which of the cars seems farthest away? Which seems closest? Of course, this is an illusion. All the cars are the same distance from you. The cars are as far away as the distance that you hold the book from your eyes.

Why do some cars seem more distant? Distant cars seem smaller to you than closer cars. If you watch a car moving toward you, it seems to get larger and larger. Very distant cars may look like dots. So how large something looks to you helps you decide how far away it is.

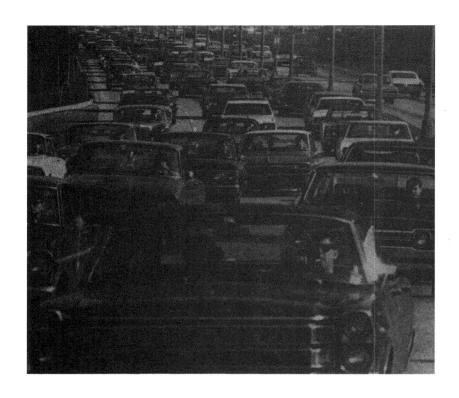

But size alone is not always enough to help you judge distance. Suppose you don't know the real size of the object. Then you may see an object as smaller either because it really *is* smaller or because it's farther away. Look at the two boxes below. Is box B smaller or more distant than box A?

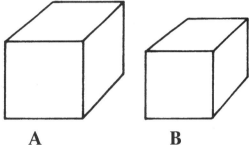

A   **B**

Suppose you show box B as being a bit higher and add a few lines as in the figure above right. Now how does it look? When lines slant toward each other, you see them as being farther away. You can see that effect in this drawing. The added lines help you see the boxes in perspective.

Lines that appear to come together in the distance are a powerful force in making you see illusions. For example, look at the drawing of a perfect square to the right. Because of the slanting lines, the top of the drawing seems farther away than the bottom. The slanting lines around the square seem to suggest that the top of the square is also farther away than the bottom. But the top and bottom of the square are the same size. So if the top is the same apparent size and yet farther away, it must be a little larger than the bottom. You can get rid of the illusion by getting rid of the surrounding lines. Use four index cards to cover the lines at the top, bottom, and sides of the square. Does it look like a square now?

Here are some other illusions caused by slanting lines that appear to vanish in the distance. Look at the two figures below. The figure to the left seems to bulge toward you in the center and away from you at the sides, the top, and the bottom. The two horizontal lines are really parallel.

The same two parallel lines are in the figure to the right. Now the slanting lines seem to meet in the distance in the center of the drawing. How do the parallel lines look different in the two figures?

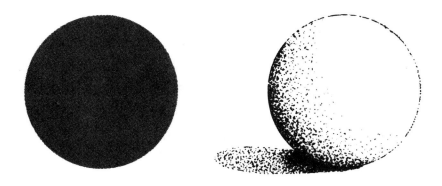

Shading and shadow also help you see distance or depth. Look at the two objects in the drawing above. One looks like a ball and the other looks like a flat circle. The ball seems to have a light shining on it from one side. The shadow and the difference in shading make you see the object as a solid ball rather than as a circle.

Looking with two eyes is a big help in finding out the shape or the distance of an object. Hold up a pencil. Close your left eye and look at the pencil with your right eye. Now look at the pencil with your left eye only. The two images are slightly different. When you look at the pencil with both eyes at the same time, the pencil looks solid.

Two photographs taken from the same distance apart as your eyes will look solid when viewed together. Perhaps you have seen some of these three-dimensional photographs. You must use a special viewer to look at them. When you look into the viewer, your right eye looks at a slightly different photo than your left eye. Your brain puts both pictures together and gives you the illusion of looking at solid objects in three dimensions.

Here is a way to show that you see a scene at a slightly different angle with each eye. Hold a pencil about one foot in front of your eyes. Look at the room beyond the pencil. Close first one eye and then the other. Notice the way the pencil appears to move against the background. Of course, the pencil isn't moving. What's moving is your point of view.

Get a friend to help you with this next experience. You will also need two pencils. Hold a pencil in each hand. Have your friend stand across the room from you. Tell your friend that you are going to start by holding one pencil closer to him or her and then move it farther away. Your friend is to tell you when the moving pencil seems the same distance away as the stationary pencil.

First let your friend try to estimate the distance of the pencils with both eyes open. Then let him or her try to guess with only one eye open. You'll be surprised at how much difference there will be when your friend views the pencils with one eye.

In spite of the fact that you use both eyes to see distance and depth, you use one of your eyes more than the other. Here's how to find out which one. Extend your arm and point your finger directly at a distant object. Now shut first one eye, then the other. You'll find that you are still pointing at the object with one eye but not with the other. The eye that you use for pointing is the one you use more.

Ask your friends to try the same experiment. You will find that some people use their right eye and some people use their left eye. It seems that just as some people are right-handed and others left-handed, some are right-eyed and others left-eyed.

6 | Brightness and Contrast

You don't see a bright object in the same way as you see a dim object. A brightly lit white object produces an image on your retina that spreads out slightly. This makes it appear somewhat larger than a dimly lit object of the same size. For example, look at the figure to the left in bright light. The white square appears larger than the black square even though they are of equal size.

In the figure to the right, the white inner circle seems larger than the black inner circle. Again, they are really of equal size.

 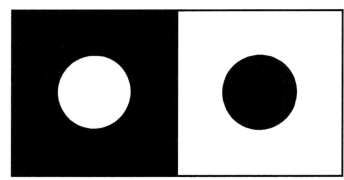

Everything looks larger if it reflects more light. An overweight person looks thinner in dark clothing than in light clothing. A brightly colored box of cornflakes seems larger than a darkly colored box. The filament of a light bulb in a flashlight appears larger when it is giving off light.

Here's how to do an experiment that shows this effect. You will need a candle, matches, and a ruler. *Caution: Perform this experiment with an adult helper.* Light the candle. Hold the ruler in front of the flame so that only the top part of the flame is visible. The ruler will appear to be notched where the bright light of the flame seems to spread out.

The background against which you see an object has a great influence on what you see. The figure to the left shows stripes of gray that are exactly the same shade. Yet

 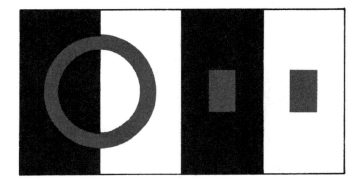

the gray on the white background looks much darker than the gray on the dark background.

The figure to the right shows some gray circles and some gray boxes that are all the same shade. How do they look to you?

If the contrast between a bright and a dim object is too

great, you will not be able to even see the dim object. On the road at night, you can't see a car behind a headlight when the headlight is shining in your eyes. When your room is brightly lit at night, someone can see in through the window glass but you can't see out through it.

Here's a funny effect that you get from brightness contrast. Look at the figure to the left. Do you see gray dots at the intersections of the white lines? If you stare at one of the dots, it may go away, but the other dots will appear darker.

In the figure to the right, you can see gray dots where the black lines intersect. Again, if you stare at one of the dots, it will disappear.

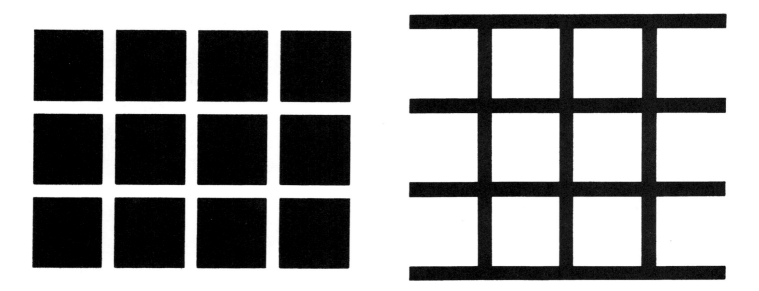

The ghostly dots that you see at the intersections may have something to do with your retina getting tired of staring at an object. Retinal fatigue can give you something called an afterimage. Look at the white crosses in the figure to the right under a bright light. Stare at them a few minutes without shifting your eyes. Then look at a sheet of blank white paper. What do you see?

Even the black print of the book that you are reading is part of an illusion. It looks darker than it really is because of the white paper on which it is printed. Look at the large letter *a*. Make a small hole in a piece of black velvet cloth. Lay the hole over part of the letter. Does the print look as dark when it is surrounded by black as it does when it is surrounded by white?

7 Color

Your eye contains two different kinds of nerve cells: rods and cones. These two types of cells have different jobs. The cones give us the ability to see colors. The rods are sensitive to shades of brightness. We use the cones more during the day and in bright light. We use the rods more at night and when the light is dim.

In the center of the retina (see page 10) are many cones and no rods. Around the outer edges of the retina, the number of cones decreases and there are more and more rods.

The tiny spot in the center of your eye that contains only cones gives you the sharpest image. If you glimpse something out of the corner of your eye that you want to see more clearly, you turn your eye so that the image of the object falls onto the central spot.

Here's how you can show that the central spot of your retina is not very sensitive to dim light. Go outside on a clear night and look up at the starry sky. Pick out one medium-bright star. Now stare directly at it without shifting your eyes. The star will dim and almost disappear because of the absence of light-sensitive rods in the center spot. But if you glance a little to the side, the star will suddenly brighten. That's because the star's image is falling on the rods around the edges of your retina.

The lack of bright light at night is the reason why everything looks gray. Sunlight is about 160,000 times brighter than moonlight. The silvery light of the moon is the result of your viewing it with color-blind rods. The color-sensing cones do not respond to the moon's dim light.

Of course, you do not see color with your eyes alone. As in every other kind of visual experience, your brain plays an important role in the colors you see.

You can show how your brain is involved in sensing colors with a device called a color wheel. Cut out a circle of white cardboard about four inches in diameter. Color half the circle bluish green and the other half red. Push a straight pin through the center of the cardboard disk. Hold the disk in the sunlight or under a very bright light, and then spin it as rapidly as you can.

The bright colors will combine with each other, and you will see a neutral or grayish tint. You can show the same thing by coloring one half of the disk greenish-yellow and the other half violet. Using a hand drill to spin the disk faster makes the demonstration work even better.

Here's more evidence of the role your brain plays in seeing color. You will need a piece of red cellophane and a piece of green cellophane. Hold the red cellophane in front of one eye and the green cellophane in front of the other eye. Now look at a sheet of white paper. You might be surprised at the result. The two color sensations are combined in your brain. You see a sheet of white paper without any trace of the red or the green.

The colors you see are influenced by the surroundings. On a piece of white paper, draw a star that looks like the illustration to the left. Color the star with an orange marker. Look at the star in dim light and then in bright light. How does the orange appear to change?

If you have different-colored bulbs such as those on a string of Christmas tree lights, look at the star in blue or green light and then in yellow or red light. Does the star look much more intensely orange in the contrasting blue or green light than in the more similar yellow or red light?

Colors affect each other when you see them together. You can demonstrate this by drawing and coloring the same orange-colored star on several sheets of paper. Color the background differently on each paper. Which colors seem to have the greatest effect on the orange? Which seem to have the least effect?

Now look at an orange star through a small hole in a piece of white cardboard. Does it look different in color and brightness than it does when you view it against its colored surroundings?

Another interesting color illusion that you can demonstrate is called an afterimage. After staring at a bright object for a time and then looking away, you will see an afterimage of the same shape and size but of a different color.

Try this. Use a bright red marker to color a square on a sheet of white paper. Hold the paper under a bright light and stare at the center of the red square for thirty seconds. Still keeping your eyes fixed at the same spot, replace the paper with a sheet of blank white paper. Keep staring at the blank paper, and in a few seconds you'll see the square reappear. Only this time the square will be bluish green rather than red.

You are seeing an afterimage of the red square. If you shift your eyes and look around the blank paper, the afterimage will fade away. It will last longer when you stare at the original image for a longer time in bright light.

If you try the same experiment but start out with a green square, the afterimage will be purplish red or pink. These color-pairs are called complementary colors. When the lights of complementary color-pairs are mixed together, the result is white light.

All lights have color, even white light. White light is really the sum of certain colored lights. Red, green, and blue light mixed together add up to white light. But when mixed in different amounts, these three colored lights can also produce any other color. Scientists call them the primary colors.

Opposite each primary color of pigment is its complementary color. For example, cyan (a kind of bluish green) is the complement of red; yellow is the complement of blue; and magenta (a kind of purple) is the complement of green. Colors in between these primaries and their complements have their own complements. Scientists and artists often use a color wheel with all the colors in a circle. From this wheel the complementary colors can easily be identified. Complementary colors are opposite each other on the wheel.

When you stare at one of a pair of complementary

colors, your eyes seem to become fatigued with that color. For example, when you stare at a red square, your eyes tire of red. When you switch over to looking at a white surface, your eyes subtract the red you were staring at, and you see its complementary color, bluish green.

You can use your knowledge of afterimages to construct some amusing posters to show your family and friends. For example, you can draw an American flag on a large white poster. But this American flag is unlike any you have ever seen. Use markers to make seven green stripes alternating with six black stripes. Color the stars black against an orange field.

Now hang the flag on a wall. Hang a blank white poster nearby. Shine a bright light on the peculiar flag and ask your friends to stare directly at it for thirty seconds. Now have your friends look at the blank poster. Amazing! They will see an afterimage of the American flag in its true colors—red, white, and blue.

Other drawings you can make for their afterimages include a purple cow, violet bananas, a green-suited Santa Claus with a black beard, and a green sunset. Experiment to see which afterimages other colors produce. Perhaps you can prepare an afterimage show for your friends and classmates.

Painters and other artists have used optical illusions since the early beginnings of art. As far back as prehistoric cave drawings, artists have tried to show the real three-dimensional world on a flat two-dimensional surface. Perspective, light and shade, contrast, and color are some of the tools that artists use to achieve their effects.

It is interesting to look at drawings or paintings and try to pick out the ways in which the artist used materials to make you see with his or her own vision. For example, look at this print of a landscape by the seventeenth-century artist Jacob van Ruisdael.

Can you tell what building materials were used in the construction of the cottage? How does the artist set the mood of the day? Notice the use of shading and line to show the difference between water and land. Despite the many years that have passed since the print was made, the scene is a familiar one that you recognize quickly.

Van Ruisdael, Jacob. *Luogo roccioso,* Alinari/Art Resource, Inc.

But look at the print made by the eighteenth-century artist Giovanni Battista Piranesi. The title of the print is *Prisons,* but no prisons such as these ever existed outside the artist's mind.

Piranesi makes you see huge and deep spaces with stone arches, timbers, and ropes. He uses perspective, light and shade, and contrasting shades of gray. Bridges and stairs seem to go no place and have no reason. You see a solid structure made of huge blocks of stone. Yet it is somehow unreal and shadowy.

Piranesi, Giovanni Battista. *Carceri d'Invenzione,* Alinari/Art Resource, Inc.

Escher, M. C. *Day and Night,* © Beeldrecht, Amsterdam/VAGA, New York Collection Haags Gemeentemuseum—The Hague.

Modern artists have gone even further with the use of optical illusions. One of the most interesting uses of different kinds of illusions is found in the works of the twentieth-century artist M. C. Escher. This is a work of his called *Day and Night.*

Look carefully at the picture and describe what you see. Do you see the white birds flying off to the right and the black birds flying off to the left? Look how the birds merge into sections of the landscape. In the center of the print, each bird is outlined by the shapes of other birds. As you look, your perceptions change.

This picture is a print by Escher called *Another World.* The scene is startling. Not only does it show a weird figure against a strange background, but directions and distances are also confused and meaningless. Which way is up or down? From what angle are you looking at the picture? Escher uses optical illusions to make you believe in impossible places. In a small area on a flat surface, Escher shows you the mind-spinning strangeness of distant universes.

Escher, M. C. *Another World,* © Beeldrecht, Amsterdam/VAGA. New York Collection Haags Gemeentemuseum—The Hague.

This picture is another print by Escher that may remind you in certain ways of the Piranesi *Prisons.* Stairs go up and down. But where do they lead? Who are the figures and what are they doing? It all depends on your point of view. When the great scientist Albert Einstein developed his theory of relativity, he made scientists see and understand in new ways. Escher tries to make us see in new ways with his own *Relativity.*

Escher, M. C. *Relativity,* © Beeldrecht, Amsterdam/VAGA. New York Collection Haags Gemeentemuseum—The Hague.

This print is also by Escher. It is called *Waterfall.* Look at it carefully. Follow the path of the waterfall all around the building. Do you believe what you see? How can water keep flowing around and around and yet downhill all the time? The illusion is so convincing that you'll have a hard time figuring out why you see it. One clue is to check the columns where they support each level.

Escher, M. C. *Waterfall,* © Beeldrecht, Amsterdam/VAGA. New York Collection Haags Gemeentemuseum—The Hague.

There are many other artists who use optical illusions in important ways in their works. This picture is a print of a painting called *Ondho,* by the contemporary artist Victor Vasarely. Changes in the size and the shape of the squares and circles and in the position of the lines make the figures appear to advance and retreat.

Vasarely, Victor. *Ondho* 1956–60. Oil on canvas, 7 ft. 2⅜ in. x 71 in. Collection, The Museum of Modern Art, New York. Gift of G. David Thompson.

Another contemporary artist who used illusions is Josef Albers. Look at his *White Embossings on Gray VIII*. Are you sure you see the figures the way you think you do? Look again.

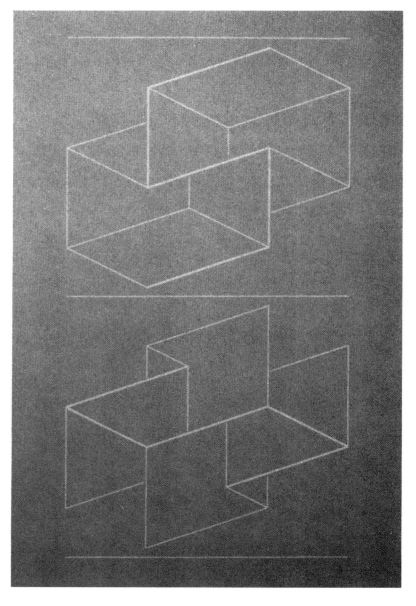

Albers, Josef. *White Embossings on Gray VIII.*
Personal collection of Kenneth E. Tyler.

Finally, this picture is an example of a form of art called optical, or op, art. It is by the contemporary artist Bridget Riley. The title is *Current.* No matter how still you keep your eyes, the picture seems to be in motion.

Riley, Bridget. *Current,* 1964. Synthetic polymer paint on composition board, 58⅛ in. x 58⅞ in. Collection, The Museum of Modern Art, New York. Philip Johnson Fund.

9 | More Optical Illusions to Try

There are lots of optical illusions that you can try out by yourself or with your friends. Here's a sampling of some that are fun.

You can make a cartoon character move very much the way animated figures do in the movies. You will need a few sheets of typing paper, a pair of scissors, a stapler or a large paper clip, and a pen or pencil. Cut thirty or forty strips of paper about 1½ inches wide by 3 inches long. Stack them neatly and staple them together along the bottom. Now, on each one of the strips, draw a picture that is just a little bit different from the one before it. For example, you might have a rocket ship moving or a figure running or jumping across the page as shown in the illustration below. Now hold the bottom of the stack firmly with your left hand. With your right hand, bend the strips backward and allow them to flip forward. You will get an illusion of motion. The rocket ship will appear to move, or the figure will appear to run or jump across the strips.

This optical illusion uses the same principle as do regular movies. Your eyes keep an image for a short time. If you see another image in quick succession, your eyes blend the images together and you see the illusion of motion. In the movies, still pictures are projected on the screen at the rate of twenty-four every second. Each still picture is slightly different from the one before, just as in your strips. You will see these still pictures with the illusion of movement.

The word *moiré* is used to describe the patterns you get when you overlap two or more similar patterns that have regular spacing. All you need to make a moiré is two metal screens or two wide-meshed nylon stockings. Hold the screens or stockings one in front of the other, as they are in the drawing above right. Turn them in different directions, as the drawing below right suggests. As you turn them against each other, you will see changing moiré patterns develop. The explanation for seeing a moiré pattern is quite complicated. But what seems to be important is the way you see the points where one line intersects another. Any kind of regular patterns superimposed atop each other will produce a moiré.

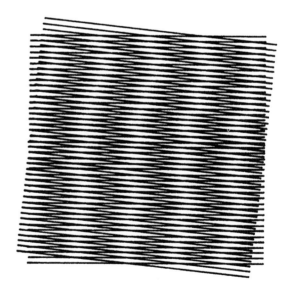

Look at the spiral in the drawing on page 62. Now revolve it. When you turn the spiral in one direction, the lines seem to move toward the center. When you turn the spiral in the other direction, the lines seem to move outward from the center. Perhaps you have seen a toy that

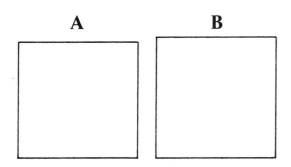

A   B

works on the same principle. When you spin the toy, the spiral on it seems to become smaller or larger depending on the direction of the spin.

Remember the impossible figure on page 8? The figure above left is an impossible triangle. Each angle is reasonable, but all the angles placed together are impossible. It looks that way because it is really a flat drawing, not a three-dimensional object. But you see it in three dimensions in an impossible way.

Look at the two figures to the left. Figure B is a perfect square with exactly equal sides. Does it look perfect? Now look at figure A. This figure is a little shorter than it is wide. Look at it side by side with the perfect square. Do you find that the unequal-sided figure A looks more equal than the perfect square B?

One of the most common optical illusions in nature is called a mirage. You may have seen a mirage while walking or riding down a street on a hot day. In the distance, you suddenly see what looks like a pool of water on the pavement. But the pool is an illusion. It keeps retreating from you as you try to reach it.

The mirage is due to changes in the atmosphere just above the surface of the ground. The ground gets very hot under a summer sun and heats the air right above it. The rising air causes changes in the direction of light rays passing through. You see these changes as ripples and movements that look like water.

These changes in the atmosphere account for the mirages of lakes in the desert and icebergs in the sea. But any more complicated mirages, such as an ice cream soda or a bathtub filled with ice water, are probably just the result of an overactive imagination.

Optical illusions are interesting and fun. Ask your family, friends, and classmates to tell what they see in an illusion. Perhaps they will suggest other illusions you can try out. You might keep a notebook containing descriptions of the optical illusions you tried and your results. Then you can see your favorites again and again!

Index